The Newest Employee of the
MUSEUM OF RUIN

The Newest Employee of the
MUSEUM OF RUIN

Charlie Clark

Four Way Books
Tribeca

FOR SASHA, THE SUN

Library of Congress Cataloging-in-Publication Data

Names: Clark, Charlie, 1977- author.
Title: The newest employee of the museum of ruin / Charlie Clark.
Description: Tribeca : Four Way Books, [2020] |
Identifiers: LCCN 2020021729 | ISBN 9781945588525 (paperback)
Subjects: LCGFT: Poetry.
Classification: LCC PS3603.L35666 N49 2020 | DDC 811/.6--dc23
LC record available at https://lccn.loc.gov/2020021729

This book is manufactured in the United States of America and printed on
acid-free paper.

Four Way Books is a not-for-profit literary press. We are grateful for the assistance we receive
from individual donors, public arts agencies, and private foundations.

This publication is made possible with public funds from the
New York State Council on the Arts, a state agency.

We are a proud member of the Community of Literary Magazines and Presses.

CONTENTS

Notes

I have a knocking woodpecker in my heart and I think I have three souls
One for love one for poetry and one for acting out my insane self
—Kenneth Koch, "Alive for an Instant"

Pseudo-Martyr

Every five years my failure as a man gets weirder.

Once, in the woods and lost, I tried to track a trail of vapor home.

That was the seventh time I legitimately thought that I might die.

Another time, in Paris, was over a bar tab in a discothèque called Le Pélican.

After that I went home and read John Donne poorly.

He wrote from convolution into convolution.

He tried to say which is preferable, to be good or destroyed.

He preferred to be destroyed.

He did not write of pelicans.

Yet I read him poorly.

So in reading him I thought of pelicans.

How they hunt by an immense falling from the air.

How long they carry the dead around inside their mouths.

How they have no notion of their strangeness.

How they would be enviable if not for this:

They are fervent but without song.

That night I dreamed of a pelican named John Donne.

This is typical of my weirdness.

It fell upon our marriage bed.

I volunteered to be the one consumed.

I sat up inside the creature's beak beside the many dead it hauled.

I tried to speak but its gullet swallowed every sound.

The dead there had devised a kind of pantomime.

I learned it soon enough.

Its every word meant *grieve.*

Grieving, alive but dead, I thought of my sweet wife.

With her in mind, I found the deadest dreadful body there.

I tore a length of its dried flesh free.

Upon that flesh I wrote these words.

With some finger bones I bored a hole through the pelican's low beak.

When we passed above our home again, I spat the message through.

It darted, ardent as an insect, into my wife's sleeping ear.

She woke then, not knowing what I'd done.

My song thrived inside her; humming always, though I was gone.

An Apple Waiting to Be Carved

In 1892 a man awoke wishing his name meant
detour on the way to pleasure because the angel

wings he sprouted in the night, though useless,
came with the most arduous requirements

for care. His neck grew long and exhausted
always having to reach his face around to peck

away the chiggers and the grit. He went through
the streets wrapped in so many gray scarves

people mistook him for a cloud. Though he was
more than just a font of gloom. He translated

Medea and *The Bacchae* into French. The scripts,
while obviously the work of an amateur,

were warmly received. Other things happened,
possibly the most important being that when he died

his bones came to rest upon an English heath.
Henry Moore, age eleven, walking lost in one brown

chill of spring, already convinced he would
never adequately render a single human face,

found the bones, mistaking them for the dead
branches of a tree that had tried in its sprouting

to turn human. It was like watching fire,
Henry in his later years said of this moment.

It was like watching fire, then becoming fire.
Suddenly you could make everything as you do burn.

Elegy to a Black Bear Head Poorly Stuffed and Mounted

Whoever did this must be
kin to that matador I saw
booed out of the arena for not
basking longer in the task.

Why else would your snout
be sewn in that hasty, ragged
line and set off-center?
Your eyes are two wool holes

with nail heads for pupils.
When I peer into the rust
of them I can't even see
an oblong version of myself.

Bear, if this is an elegy,
you ought to have a name
more specific than Bear.
Not that you care, but I am

going to call you Lou Reed.
Because whoever made him
quit working with the face
still a bunch of half-done

lumps of clay. Also because
he's one whose output
illustrates how art is not
getting what you want.

Art is getting only what
he decides to give you.
Lou Reed, you give me
the impression that a career

spent so close to killing
only becomes more intolerable
as it goes on. Even if
one is elegant, thoughtful,

and perfect at it, after
a while one's limbs are
going to revolt. Lou Reed,
this is what I think. When

the taxidermist hammered
those nails into your eyes
it was the final step
in his coming to hate

anyone who could look
at his life's work and not
regret being human.
Once he finished up with you,

he left his studio. He walked
to a lake where a pair of swans
were doing circles. He liked
the elegance of their bodies

on the water. He gave thanks
that the way they mate for
life makes these creatures
no less adamant and cruel.

First he fed the swans
the crackers he had brought.
When those were gone
he let them have his hands.

Ranch Hand Blasting Pantera in the Cow Pasture

To their bones it must seem like strange wind.
He's listened with them for three years now.
The only effect it's had is that when the songs cut off
he hears a ringing rather than their murmur.
It's that much less rebuke. He thought it would
move through the herd more like when he drives
among them a few bars faster than he should,
headlights like wet blotter shining on their hides.
Only in the low and whirl of such privacy
does he watch his hands become two thick pistols
giving back to heaven its little bolts of thanks.
Walking through the pasture, the fact that
he knows people who claim to see loved ones'
eyes stare back continues to confuse him.
He stares and sees the colors of the uniforms
it was, in a past he did not disclose on his application,
too often his duty to make clean. He stares and sees
the shale of rainclouds, or smoke rising from some
far grass patch whose location is vague but no less
difficult for him to believe in beyond the rudiments
of its burning. He stares and sees the illiterate
that for three years now he has dreamed of,

sees the color of his tongue as he receives his death
papers, papers he understands immediately
even though he cannot read, because they are a king's
words, meaning they have been delivered
sealed in a gaudy, wine-dark wax, meaning they are
already everywhere, meaning you can burn them,
you can burn the paper or the vellum or whatever
they arrived on, you can burn that iota of
the kingdom and still its words will go on ringing.
Each night for three years now he has dreamed
of the illiterate doomed by the king's pleasure.
Each morning for three years now he has woken
to flanks of stale cornbread, these farting cows,
and this music that he loves. *This love*, he caws,
slapping the closest one, seeing how well
this, the latest, most-benign form of hardness
he has tried on works. After three years
of appraising it, he knows it never will. Three years.
Bleak to bleak to bleak. Bone to bone to bone.
He believes his kingdom will never deliver
him from these cows. Their days together
comprise layers of gray, wet grass and his high

mockeries. As loudly as he can make it
go, syllable after syllable, the word *re-*
spect tattoos the air as though the air were an eager
wall of flesh. Call it pleasure. In the flesh of the ear
this breath that lingers even as it vanishes.

Giving Stuff Up

One friend decided to forego sugar for a month. Another the word *wept*.
A third quit therapy in favor of praising the aubergine tinge in the clouds

that served as backdrop to the tree limbs falling through his mother's yard.
Sometimes I want to give up living by lists and information, yet I still want

to tell you how this morning I watched a man launch some kites on a beach.
When the wind had a good hold of one, he'd take a lighter to its string.

He must have doused them in gas beforehand because the flames ran fast,
caught the kites, and the ensuing red shreds frothed upon the vapors.

Listen, if you've never heard about the time Shakespeare got drunk,
snuffed the candelabra, and in its dark tried to wrestle every member of his cast,

that's because damage had paired with sorrow even then. That fiasco was nothing.
Where he lived, the wind could change direction and for two whole weeks

the house would smell like gas. That's half of how he came up with the mist
for *Macbeth*'s witches. The other half was theft. After the headaches passed,

everything in those fumes seemed like a dream. Even weasels lolled in the grass,
like pets built out of licorice. I don't know how he invented the words

gust or *radiance* in such haze, but I'm glad for their perfection. The modern match
was perfected in 1805. Before that, every burn meant tinder, flint, and steel.

So that man igniting kites still could have done it by the Thames in 1597,
although I like to imagine whatever material he'd have used to build them

proved clumsy in the river's wind, every flaming body rising no more
than a few yards before it plunged. Or maybe the fault lay with the wind. Listen.

Seeing them through the window, Shakespeare claimed the first one as his son.
The rest became the angels he renounced, hearing thereafter only human tongues.

The Words in a Same Poem All Mean the Love Thing

Summertime is a castle of long white grass.
Anything can make me think of you.
Squares of sunlight burning on my chest.
Hoarders marathons close-captioned at the gym.
At night, when I'm counting the books that I can bear to part with,
something I do
under the auspices of cleaning house,
nothing ever actually leaves the shelves.
Words are made to accumulate, like plaque in one's ventricles.
Even the idiot who runs my heart knows this.
Solitary man, he won't say it but he lives for your company.
The hope is that he dies of it.

Cut me some slack. I don't have a death wish,
however much I may circle back to it
as a subject. As a subject, it's tied with love, painters,
Replacements songs, and the garbage I see when biking.
Life is full of candy wrappers bleached white under the sun.
I still mistake half of them for butterflies drunk in gutters.
English is the only means I have to show this.
Caravaggio, in hell, must not be too jealous. He had oils and Italy.
Light, therefore, let him render the unspeakable.

Almost every morning I stare directly at the sun.

Reeling, I go, blind beneath its radiance.

Kicking each pale letter of the world in place.

Fundamental Attribution Error

I am thankful my ears
merely ring, that they are
not two pilfered slips
of marble discovered

in the glove compartment
of the newest employee
of the Museum of Ruin,
whose fetish to speak

softly into stone he did not
disclose on his application.
If his manager were a kind
person—and what person

who catalogs ruin for
a living isn't at least patient
with imperfection—
he would be kinder than

the part of me that imagines
how this story's trajectory
involves squad cars and any
of several ways the thief

winds up with a banshee
in his brain, a phrase
that tastes decidedly unlike
the dirt that filled first

the mouth and nostrils
and then each of the thief's
ears when the police mashed
his head repeatedly into the ground.

They thought doing so was just
the beginning of retribution,
which is a kind of justice common
but ill-suited to human existence.

To the thief, whose brain
would soon start hissing
the word *criminal* at the image
of itself hanging in the mirror

on the barnacled wall
of its one room, the brutality
was as much inevitable as it was
an opportunity to say good-

bye to the endless and unwearied
stones inside the earth, to feel
in the ground's looseness
how they had already begun

to forgive him. That the world
will not forgive him should be
obvious. See the way it lets
the word *criminal* persist inside

him for the span of time
it keeps him away. If you want
to imagine it, imagine
permanent orange internal lightning

bolts because *orange* is the closest
a name for a color comes to *damage*.
Then imagine, in time, the thief
let back out in the world;

imagine him entering the thicket
of trees just behind his mother's
house (where else do you think
he'd live?), imagine him

digging in the dirt there
for a rock to talk to.
Imagine him working by hand
whole feet down without

uncovering a single stone,
just mounds of soil
and the trench his desperation
built. Imagine the volume

of what he does not find.
Imagine his mother standing
at her back door, a mug of tea
pressed against her temple,

having watched her son
slip into the greenery
for the purpose of she knows
not what, and how the bleating

thing that fills her then is her
wonder at how deep into
the trees her son must go
before she can say he's gone.

What the Backyard Will Not Give

Not doubloons.
Not carrots.
Not trees.
Therefore
not shade.
Therefore
not rest.
Not even
the dream of it.
So not grace.
Not even green.
It will give dust.
It will give grease.
It will give up
the greasy
fettered feathers
of birds busily
becoming heat.
But not worms.
Not enough,
at least.
Nor the lush
promise
their thriving

might provide.
Therefore
not daisies.
Nor tulips.
Therefore not
the eye's relief.
It will give haze.
It will give glass.
Flung in two
thousand
arcing shards.
It will give
a modern history
of trash. Cups
and plates
of polystyrene
and pine-scented
hand-sized
cardboard trees.
It will give
my daughter
rashes, burns,
and bleeds.
So it will

give grief.
Enough to
chafe on
in the slotted
August light
and breeze.
And stones.
It will
give stones.
One whole
rainbow's
ragged range.
Shucked
by boots.
By fingers.
By the trowel's
buckled blade.
Enough
to stack.
To study,
catalog,
and grade.
Though
doing so

will not bless

this place.

Though I

do—despite

myself—

still wish

to know

their names.

Mr. Dreamy

Now when I see a night
that's weak with clouds,

it makes me nervous.

All those rings
wrenched around the moon.

There are rhymes I don't remember

that say whatever it is
such a sky's rising

supposedly portends.

Whatever it is, I feel it.
Sometimes I wish

the night were unnecessary.

Most nights that I feel that way
I feel the same

about day come daybreak.

See the sun bleeding
through the trees? Not being

a sailor doesn't make you

any safer from it. I used to think
being left-handed meant

I was more likely to die

in a car wreck. Turns out
the biggest risk is living.

There is a grimness

to that thought; something
shallow and permanent.

When I want to be

better than that,
I give myself

one of Whitman's catalogs

to chew on. It doesn't last,
that first, capacious bubble of patience.

However well he may have

wandered and adored it,
Whitman knew

the world is a livid vale of dust,

also that it's insane
with blood, and he never even

wept in West Virginia.

When snow
surprised everyone in late

April in New Jersey, 1890,

did Whitman's neighbors
roll their eyes

at all of his raw praise?

Even if they weren't farmers,
they likely knew

what damage spring snows can do.

Did he? One book I'm reading
makes the claim that

"Whitman disliked farming

with some passion."
In my one year

as a farmhand I laid fire pots

between orchard lines
whenever it would snow.

Everything about those hours—

the limbs' frigid,
fractal beauty, briefly

outgrowing my discomfort

with the open—
I detested and desire.

Even sipping schnapps

between the rows, how
the darkness gave everything

the gauzy, aquatic depth

of the impersonal
and alluring. Going through,

setting down the tiny burning bowls,

I was as slow about that
as I was everything. My boss

called me Mr. Dreamy

and meant it
as an insult. I haven't

gotten over it so much

as tried to sculpt my life
such that my being

dreamy isn't going to cost

anyone's bottom line.
One harvest day that year

I forgot which way

the road knifed and flipped
the truck

and walked away.

When the ambulance arrived,
I smiled and tried to wave it by.

When my boss arrived

he threw a wrench at me.
It was dark by then.

I'd been sitting there for hours.

The sky was clear.
The moon

blew through it.

The road below
was lit bright

with our tremendous apples.

My whole life
I have wondered

what's become of me.

Inheritance

I am descended from a people
who used dictionaries
to wipe blood up off the floor.
If you think that's insane,
look into your family tree.

If you don't find that dragon
Columbus roiling in his gold
filigree, keep looking.
Someone set his neighbor's
house on fire because

the neighbor would not
let him in the door. I am
descended from a people
who threw women into water
and when those women

turned into the spewing
towers of Hawaii, my people
ventured there off-season,
drenched in sunscreen,
their noses squinched up

at strange odors. I have
visited the cathedrals
they built to keep the memory
of those women at bay.
Their roofs are now all open

air, and I'm fine with that,
though it's unfortunate
their makers couldn't see them
like this, goats passing through,
birds shitting on everything,

because they could not have
looked any better new.
I am the fulcrum of a history
built on fear and best intentions.
I am the predecessor

of a people who know
scrubbing off the bird shit
will only accelerate decay,
yet they spend their mornings
arched up to it, whistling

every falling side wall clean.
I am the predecessor of a people
who will hold a bent stick
into the air and go walking
whichever way it leads—

a trick I pass down to let them
seem less lost. It is not a right,
though for them it will happen
like it were one: irrefutable,
brutal, god-given, free.

Carrying My Brother to the Ambulance

This close, I for the fourth decade notice how
beautiful I find the stark black lashes of his eyes.

It's autumn—after autumn, actually—everything
awash in the given plenty of spent leaves. Ice

in the air despite the sun. A few bars of something
bracing I can't quite place grace the whole of the cradle

that we've made. I slow as if to ask *what song is that*?
I can't stop noticing, which is already a kind of asking.

Which is one way to have a story go on without end.
Another way to keep a story from ending

is never to start telling it. My brother's silent,
split, spilt, bruised, half-buried in his milk, gone

red at the tongue, orange at the eye. So entwined
and still I don't once stagger in the dirt.

I still have my brother. My hands know this
by the weight. As if the worth of life were knowing.

I never knew I could carry him. Now it's another story.
Once I caught his front teeth with a bat.

Once I saw a dog chasing a child and I tackled it.
I didn't think of fear until its body was here,

livid in my arms. By then there was no time. Now,
out of my hands, my hands grate air like they are the place

in the earth where roots continue to turn dirt into themselves
while above a blade has clipped the bloom completely.

My last conversation with Mary Jane Bailey

was about the taste of buckshot in baked swan.
I wanted to remember more, but couldn't.

Someone suggested bloodletting. Someone else
suggested several hours of ghost talk. I suggested

nothing. Picture this. Picture her with a rifle
posed beside a Buick. Picture her taking someone's

stray blast in the chest while quail hunting in 1942.
Picture how she dressed her wounds and drove

herself over hours of knocking Idaho backroads
to the nearest doctor's house. There was a war on,

after all. (Though when isn't there a war on?)
Every act amounted to a sacrifice. Tell me, Mary,

which of my actions counts as preparation for life
during wartime. Yes, the inconsistent stretches

and push-ups. Yes, the quiet watching in the night.
No, the amount of toilet paper I use each week.

No, all my fawning over music. Not even Napalm Death,
Machine Gun Etiquette, or "Life During Wartime."

No, the writing of poems. When Creeley called Koch
lightweight—or rather when I came across this

while reading someone's gloss on the poetry wars—
it sounded like Creeley believed his poems

could chop wood, start fires, inflict wounds.
In poetry the goal is always to inflict wounds.

So say the vagaries of some strange muse. I do
terrible things and claim I'm only following orders.

Picture these stanzas leavened with dead elephants.
Picture the mad man setting fire to the tree.

Picture yourself. Picture this misfortune.
To be alive in words other than your own.

How Death Is a Hole in the Ground That Dirt Can Only Cover (or, In Her Letters, Emily Dickinson Would Sometimes Refer to Death as Michigan)

It was for closure that I came down into the valley to see the thing you were.

෧

The whole time I tried to think of flowers, but never settled on a single type.

෧

I read somewhere after, or heard someone say, or maybe just decided for myself:

Because it is a sloppy thing, in grief we give ourselves permission to be both greedy and indiscrete in ways we might not understand or like.

And yet we do it, loudly and a lot.

෧

Greedy and indiscrete like the priest who after a lifetime of service retires by making his home in the village square and shouting the confessed sins of every passerby.

෧

42

When word came, Sasha and I were waking up, watching winter morning light play upon the one writhing whisker of the catfish in the Teraoka print Sasha had taped up on the wall,

and the few fine bristles sprouting from the pit of the arm of the girl so languidly wrapped around the fish amid the prim white whips of the waves,

and how the sun made both their tendrils come alive and shine.

ℛ

In the silence after, while I was online buying tickets,

Sasha mentioned how in her letters Emily Dickinson would sometimes refer to death as Michigan.

ℛ

On the plane I listened to John Fahey's *The Transfiguration of Blind Joe Death* on repeat and the only thing I didn't hear in his guitar was death, for which I was thankful, it being mostly impossible for me to watch from inside a plane as its wings cut through the bright

carpet of the clouds and think of anything but death.

∾

Except maybe heaven.

∾

Then, Michigan.

∾

A rushing that took hours to complete.

∾

In descent the world reduced to a paltry few particulars yet still so vague.

∾

All the usual darkness, the wood fire droning formally, quiet piles of rugs and snow.

&

And bunches, bunches of white daisies.

&

Seeing you, rouged, uncanny, blue, I found you were not what you were.

&

Nothing but a strangeness in the room about which there was nothing we could do.

What the Dying Said to Me in the Dream Where I Became the Dying

I hope heaven is like Texas in the fifties,

right down to all the petty bribes.

When my first love died,

all year my hands smelled of gasoline.

Each day's new pall of snow

burned back to swarming blacktop gray.

Grief, I determined, is most constructive

when you channel it through scorn.

When my second love died I started painting birds.

After fifteen years of studies my hands flitted like two wings.

I've flown this state so many times

and found nothing lustrous here.

Nothing but grief in circulation.

No matter what, don't bury me in Michigan.

Antonyms for Proteus

1. The myth of Proteus

puts all its dynamism in the wrong place.

Let's make Proteus a stone and the adventurer the one to flash and
shudder once he gets his hands on the old god's body.

When finally Proteus cracks and there's no miracle, no inner geode
glowing, the adventurer mutters an unheard bitter word or two and
throws the broken stone into the sea.

There the parts don't rejoin.

The sea covers them in salt and spends centuries crushing them.

*2. Wanting to Know What Words the Adventurer Said, I Try to Get a Better
Sense of Him*

Here are the synonyms for *Adventurer* available in my computer's
dictionary/thesaurus:

Explorer
Voyager

Buccaneer
Swashbuckler
Fortune-Teller
Traveler
Entrepreneur
Investor

Reading those, I feel the progress of history, from ocean ropes to white shoes and corporate-sponsored deep-water pollution.

3. The Sound of the Ocean

In every recording of the ocean that I've listened to, no matter what the quality, my favorite part is when the surf recedes.

Hearing it, the word I think of is *declension*.
In Greek the meaning is grammatical.

Something like the way a noun may vary to identify its number or gender.

Revelation through change.

So it's fitting for the sea, and for Proteus to be a god of it.

In English the word's far more limited.

It means failing.

4. Antonyms

One antonym for *declension* is *morality*.

There's no antonym for *Proteus*.

Though *Antonym* does sound like it could be the name of the Greek adventurer in the myth I guess I'm writing.

The one who, young and eager and not knowing that a god can only be itself or nothing, sought and found the stone Proteus and then threw it in the sea when it didn't turn to riches.

It was his only quest and he came home with nothing but the sound of the ocean forever breaking *failure* in his brain.

5. Autobiography

All writing is a reflection of the self.

In this way I am Proteus as much as I am Antonym as much I am dictionary/thesaurus as much as I am salt or corporate-sponsored pollution as much as I am the sound of the ocean and all the declensions it conjures and contains.

In that everything in these words is my own doing.

6. Everything

Everything is a very large word.

Rather than *everything*, let's say *something*.

Something sounds more manageable, like you can hold it in your hands the way you can hold a dictionary or a stone.

What you cannot hold is the sound of the ocean, which is probably why that's where beauty starts.

7. Now that I've introduced beauty and the second person

here's a revelation.

I am the adventurer gone out into the world of silence, looking for a way to break it and come back to you rich and well received.

It is curious, wandering so deep into silence and thinking that a word will be there at the end of it.

8. What I Found While Looking for the End of Silence

Nothing but a reflection of the self.

In that something in these words is my own doing.

In that by *something* what I mean is *everything*.

In that by *doing* what I mean is *fault*.

In that by *fault* what I mean is I'm the one who's cracking.

In that I'm a stone, even with all these words I'm churning.

In that the only time I'm certain of a word is when I'm certain that it's wrong.

In that the best word I've said today by far is *ocean*.

In that you are like the ocean.

In that just thinking of you crushes me.

9. *What an Antonym Cannot Undo*

I am the crushed pieces of a deity thrown by hand into the sea.

I am Antonym and all of his regret.

I am searching for a miracle of a word that will undo this.

10. *Miracle*

Maybe *miracle*'s the word and my tongue is Proteus.

Maybe that's why it sometimes feels so much like stone.

When I hold it in between my fingers and whisper *miracle* the word I hear is *marigold*.

11. Marigold *Has No Antonym*

Not *swashbuckler*, not *entrepreneur*.

Not *declension, failure,* or *biography*.

Not *deity* or *silence*.

Not even *rose* or *lily*.

All it has are its parts, two separate pledges of abundance the English tongue transforms to one.

Just to think them makes the darkest stone inside me glow.

12. *What* Flower *Is a Synonym For*

Let's let Proteus be nothing.

Let's leave the divine out of this.

Let's have you be the water and I'll be the field of flowers blooming close beside it.

Or you can be the field and I will be the water.

The order of our being doesn't matter.

So long as there is something to nourish daily,

like a marigold, waving.

The Gypsies Singing Goodbye to Their Child

When we stole you
we also took the kitchen's largest pot
and three round loaves of bread.
The pot you slept in sometimes.
The loaves became your favorite toys.
One you tore in half and used as a coconut
to recount for us Monty Python's *Holy Grail*.
But we read the papers. We're not such fools.
That's why we've put you in this park.
Your front tooth we pulled so we'd at least have something.
It's the only hurt we hope will never heal.
We take turns sucking it at night.
Each time it grows smaller, less distinctly bone.
I don't know what we'll do when it's all gone.

The Loves in a Word Poem All Mean the Same Thing

Consider this an admission of deficiencies.

How I can't identify a single tree.

After three drinks they all look like live oaks growing.

Reading John Donne is even worse.

Less analysis than a bloodletting ensues.

I used to think I could make a name for myself this way.

Exploring wounds like the lousy bites of love.

Consider this an admission of intimacies

laid out against advice from counsel.

Ah, what a trifle is the heart,

rocking in the cradle of my chest,

k-holed recounting each blemish it's bestowed.

Should I start explaining myself?

Appropriation seemed necessary at the moment.

Sometimes one must veer wherever one is veering.

Here's a different admission.

At sixteen, on a Chevron station's bathroom wall, I scribbled

Søren Kierkegaard quotations as though they were my own.

(Under no circumstance would I say that I've matured.)

Now what was that but a veiled appeal for love?

Winters then were a sleepy purple hell

except for a few clear views of constellations.
Should the future build a time machine, I would
take it only here and now, to this, our very strand of days.

Cocktail Parties in the City of the Dead

1.

Well, I still can cut my finger on the pull tab of a beer
though there's no one here to curse at about it.
And regardless it is summer.
Or at least it's always blazing in the periphery.
And here comes Duncan, grinning like a ghost.
The concrete path he walks along ripples
like abs do during laughter.
Even after hours of discussing the rickshaws
and disappointment scattered through our dreams
I can't tell which is doing the other the favor
of standing out here in this heat.
Each of us, when he gets home, will put a hand into the fire.

2.

Always the talk of how the other side's insane.
Always the solution comes in varying degrees of fire.
Always the children herded off and minded
by the one mother too soft in the head to know
the guests and her husband are just as happy
not to have her sweet birdsong lilt around

as they are to be without their kids a while.
Always comes an hour when the faces start to seem
like those on dolls made from sun-dried apple cores.
Always someone ends up passed out in the flowers
and how the dew and sunlight cover him
the next morning is the closest nature comes to mercy.

3.

In the moments where the conversations die
the hostess blesses the noise of late arrivals.
Even here that remains fashionable.
Each time she opens a fresh bottle of the best thing left.
There are so many bad ways to stave off fire,
so few easily done well alone.
Think of Nero however late into the night offering his niece
as the bowl from which some just-arrived senator
he's going to off in two weeks anyway
can have a bit of honey or crushed berries
mixed with the uncorrupted snow he's sent his runners
back into the mountains to gather freshly fallen heaps of.

Inventory

Shed skin of sweet potato in hand.
Feeble orange water trolling to the elbow's
crook. Here I have arms, have elbows,

have hands, each a blessing I assume.
Here I have the blessing of my blood
to use them. The specific little split blade

I peeled these three odd tubers with.
And another, simpler one on hand to dice them.
Here I have more tools: pan, oil, sage, stove,

spatula of pale, hard-worked bamboo.
Here I have my wife, the fresh, blunt
wonder of our child tucked into the table,

ready to eat what tonight I am preparing.
Mother somewhere east, relieved, sipping
with large red berries under the earlier-

setting eastern sun one of those fine
green lucent wines whose particles,
coarse or crisp, haunt the nose and tongue

with the precision of the first bite into
autumnal apple meat. All these things
in a life directed toward these things.

It is so unlikely, yet inevitable, yet for that
no less shattering on arrival. This compilation.
The light, untouchable spanning of our lives.

Yet—or is it so—most likely it is so—
so still the hairs of my heart. Still burnt.
Still bleached. Still raised red and splitting.

After Catullus

Wretched Charles! You have to stop this nonsense.
Suffering is not a philosophy any more than rain is.
Rain, however, will yield you grasses and mosquitoes.
However much you rely on words like *fragrant,*
judicious, and *depending,* a horse neck stuck in razor
wire does not equal splendor. Now watch how,
despite the rain, despite the horse flies and better
clover growing away there by the barn, the other
palomino wanders your way and with its tongue
like a wet scepter begins to lick the wounds
on its entangled mate. The gentleness of that
action, that bright live meat's unfurling and retreat—
do not stick your hand in such business. Beauty
doesn't need you, not even to commend it.

♣

Amateur Hour (What Do Sad Songs Remind You Of?)

The clouds here are beautiful in the manner of my wife's hands.
They are pleasures with strange limits, and change color quickly.
In this way, they are like most beautiful things. Take songs.

In the car, when my wife turns the volume knob it's to make the sadness louder.
During the commercials or the jockey chatter after, I worry I'm depressed.
But just because I might be depressed doesn't mean I'm serious.

To be serious is to have something unwavering inside you.
And, oh, how I waver. I'd write anything so long as it was beautiful.
It's beautiful to touch either of my wife's hands.

My wife's hands are warm as flagstones set out beneath the sun.
When I touch them the ringing in my ears becomes the tuning of viola strings.
I think it was something like this that made André Breton write "Free Union."

But his enumerations get tedious. I'll limit mine to my wife's hands, then.
My wife's hands invented the word *abode*. When she folds them,
my wife's hands are tighter than the onion where all time goes.

One day it snowed and my wife put her hands inside the snow.
They came out flush as the blood in the heart of a swan.
When she put them to my face I could not feel my tongue.

Dead American Christmas Ghazal

It is difficult to live without once picturing god
Or one's hand as the contours of a gun

The perfect circle of the *o* that will not be unwound
It loops through *hole* and *moan* and *gone*

The dead do not get a holiday season though
We make the nights here glow like a heaven shot through

One's thoughts of the dead shine like Charon's pennies
They shoot through me like *god* out of a gun

It is difficult to picture the dead as nothing
Even this long after they are gone

O Charon is close enough to Charles
My first memory is finding where she kept the gun

Rimbaud's Father

Once, in Algeria, wild dogs
ate the wooden fore-wheel

of a woman's pushcart
while he and his fellow

infantrymen looked on,
a half-dozen of them

having commandeered her
porch for napping. Some

things are inevitable. How
he tried to help her clean

the pulp up after, how
something in the slobber,

the thickness of it coating
the wood, slowed him.

Each scrap white as chicken
meat after the cleaver

and the peeling and the rinsing
in cold water. He knew

men who bragged about
eating their lieutenant's

thighs after weeks trapped
in cold mountains. He knew

it was mostly lies and that
it would be their only legacy.

He knew to call the dogs
charms sent to assure him

he would survive this
and that he was not destined

for greater things. So when
one dog came back, mottled,

prancing, sharp cowlick
of its jaw angled high

to keep the rough strip
of wheel it mouthed from

dragging, one of the soldiers
shot it. It bled out howling

and they let it. Soon after,
another soldier torched

the woman's house. He cut
for himself a swatch of her

curtain. No secret to see
in the elegant little turnstiles

of its embroidery. History
is dainty. Even panic can

seem quaint there. He knows
what the future has

no use for; he's no different
than the acres of his father's

failing orchards, his hours
itching the harvest in,

the bland-to-bitter paste
they made of all its ripeless figs.

Pleasure Seeker, Spurned, Watching Sea Birds on the Beach at Dawn

First saying

     plover

if only so

the mouth

can linger

on the *o*

     can imagine

it an egg

coming delicately

whole out of

the soft hold of

the mouth

     then

for the idea of

lover mispro-

nounced

     making

the egg

a lover's gift

     spoken

     moaned

     stolen

by a lover's

lover's fingers

beneath this
bloody splash
of morning
shadows
        of
what in shadow
could be
a plover's nest's
stray tines
                or rope

                or vines

                or in
the complicating
shadows of
the mind
a spool of ser-
pent bodies
sprung new-
born and hungry
from the ocean
and in this
light an over-
stippled nightmare
white

each by
instinct already
whipping toward
the dunes
      hissing
over whose
pleasure it will
be to hollow
out the body
of the *o*
      to crush
the plover
      to have it
over every other
creature their
heaving eager
tongues discover

A Bird, Perhaps, or What Was Once a Bird

Love, this death looks like Florida.
Odd, wind-flapped squelch at the end

of things, where there's enough creeping
from the wet and light to justify your fears.

I want to believe it was a bird, though
it's conceivable that it wasn't a bird,

conceivable that until it broke open it didn't
live on wind and a cache of strangers'

cast-off melon rinds. It's conceivable that,
rather, someone, after a night of stewing

several large oranges and carrying the clear
crystal bowl of punch up the street the next day,

was by some strangeness smothered, was stricken,
was taken, was assumed, or offed, or whatever

is the word that would have that bowl and body
gone, that would leave on these cobbles

only all this pulp, now time-burnt, decayed,
delivered now, turning into the obtuse yawning

map of Florida. But I want to believe it was
a bird. I want to believe it was a bird because

they are small and the grief small dead things
provoke is sharp but brief. I am sorry

for this cruel wish, but I want my life to outlast
bitterness. I want to believe it was just a bird,

this flat black mash of the sun's ministry
I toe, looking to turn some evidence.

If I find a feather, I will tell you that it sang.
If that helps, I will tell you everything I know.

Devil Makes an Erotics of the Sun

Here now a sense of burning in the rigging of the air.

What, after so long as agent of the untouchable,

what. He has hauled not brightness. Not on his own

flickered lizard grin. Not one such penchant as this,

slack-gold, sudden, and unanimous. He calls up

the shade of Hafiz here to beggar out some habits.

What else can Hafiz say to be but crushed; what

to do but raise a swarm of bees, thicken the heart

with them, and then eat the honey they have battered.

His fingers dream of fire like ten lit candle wicks.

Each carves in the vapor's glint its own slow O.

O, they hum. Or else exhale. Some heated ceaseless

reap of breathing. Here he can't confine the wagging

tulip of his tongue. *Gentle, brightness; burn me into singing.*

These Are the Insects

Not birds, not crickets,
not even the random
spastic chatter of squirrels
quarreling across dead leaves;
there is nothing singing
from the trees, and the books
as I choose to remember
them suggest that should
be unsettling rather than
evidence of peace. And trees
is a misnomer for the way
the dozen or two shoots
of bamboo slough limply
forward in the wind like
each is a child late for a bus
he does not particularly
want to catch because
he would just as soon go on
listening to the red thing
the fever did inside his ears,
would rather with a hose
and a spoon make mud
bricks in the little shed-
veiled section of his uncle's

garden. Even at eleven
he knows he should be
ashamed that his desires
are this small and involve
dirt on his underbelly,
and he hasn't even
heard of the death
drive yet, or Wittgenstein's
blackened finger ends
proposing what must
be, let alone Li Po, that sub-
lime drunk, who crum-
pled into a moony, mud-
lit scrim of pond, then
woke to find the hard
sheen of the afterlife
bearing down, as well as
a trio of pigs politely
asking whether they could
begin to eat what his body
still obtained, the pigs
pointing to the rice-
like line of maggots already
starting in on his pale

legs. Poor Li Po, dead,

quite consciously,

despairing in heaven's

sudden mud and reeds,

with no heart to tell

the pigs he still loves

his body—wastes,

instead, the morning

hovering inches above

himself, watching, thinking:

really, these are the insects

that would destroy us,

and they don't even sing.

What Tongues Are Given

1. Our Father Cannot Soothe His Mind by Cogitating on the Origin of "Ecstasy"

The Latin
the church taught
me tells me
the root is Greek:
ek = outside;
stasis = standing,
or more simply
standing outside the self.
Always the best
explanations
involve a body.
It's why Christ
in all his blood
and bearing is
such an exquisite
model. I am
outside in
the field of
my body
observing it
and what it

feels. What it
feels is the ripe
course of wind
through this
lush field
full of chalk-
white stone
shards cropping
like the flesh
of my beloved's
ankle through
the lengthy
blue slit
of cloth it is
her habit
always to
have on when
striding past
the yawning
feckless span
of attention
in which I am
trying to jot
one more

week's devotions.
I see it and
am out in
a field weeping,
my hands
beside
themselves,
shaking
thanks upon
the bright
immaculate
flesh of stones.

2. Our Mother Kneeling, Not Praying

Lord father,
I want my knees
to press into
the body of
a meadow
beside the flush
length of that
sweet man.
I want my lungs
to rip. I want,
lord father,
old master
of my days
and nights,
to take
the hymn I
promised you
I would make
my life into
and give it to
him instead.
I want to be,

lord father,
to be rooted,
broken into
blooming
by this good
man of yours,
by his hands
and the nervous
cache of
devotions
his soft tongue
holds. Lord
father, I want
this. I am
decided.
I am not,
lord father,
asking for
your help.
Neither,
hear me,
lord, your
blessing, or
permission.

3. By Its Very Nature, God's Commentary
on This Cannot Rise above the Solipsistic

The

most

regrettable

fact

about

omniscience

is

the lack

of an

interior

in

which

a thing

that

was

not

suddenly

might

be

  linger

  let

alone

turn

requisite

      love

      breath

      the slightest

squinted

reflex

of

shared

glee

4. Our Father, behind a Door That Will
Not Give, Considers the Word "Give"

The Vikings
must have
had a hand
in it, those
furies I come
down from,
if only by
softening
the first syllable
conquered
Saxons uttered
the moment
they saw
the wood
of their last
locks fail.
Think of
the storms
those marauders
beat through
for the promise

of a wife's
mulled wine.
Three weeks
out of a decade
of the good
lord's work,
here I sit
suited in
this room
the soft, aged
blue of dolphin
fin, locked
as a paradox.
What the monks
soothed in
the Nordic
blood with books
and the more
cautious accretion
of time
I thought
would yield
me a life.
It did. Here,

or there, now,

two blocks

from this

jammed door,

a bride

to break

a door for

waits for

me among

red flowers.

A priest

in love

is a man

more cautious

than a badger

but no less

ardent.

The one

thing I do

well is give

of myself.

Forgive me,

father, if

my terms
keep changing,
like the world.
Like the world
I always have
more to give.
This wood
creaking
beneath
the weight of
me, beneath
the world
of what
I want,
this wood
singing like
a benediction.
I thank
the good
world for
the brevity of
its restraints,
how like

breath, like
a body,
I feel it
beneath me—
hand to
god—give.

5. Beside the Chapel, Our Mother
Lingers in Carnations

I love

the tongue

the lord

has made

me, love

the taste of

my man's

tongue

upon mine.

When our

kissing ends

I see his

work

between

his cheeks

like a creature

trying

to claw

itself from

knotted cloth.

That thing
would have
drowned
had I not
intervened.
The lord
I loved had
however
many tongues,
each a flame
by contrast
gorgeous,
ecstatic,
dumb.
The good
lord made
flesh,
starting with
my man.
      My
man
    my
god
    the

cloth
I want
him
out of—

Desire

This is desire in the bounty of the sun.

Simply, I want to put my hand inside your mouth.

Simply, it is not that simple.

I blame my indiscretion on the sun.

(It is so easy to blame something as grand and distant

and yet as vital as the sun.)

After winter, I am not accustomed to its long shining.

It makes all my inclinations seem amiable. Advisable.

It makes the wrong words come out of my mouth.

I want to put my hand inside your mouth.

I want your words to pass through my hand

so it can feel what it's like to make them.

I want to put my hand inside your mouth.

I want it to come back slavered.

The Things in a Poem All Mean the Same Word Love

Sometimes I wish I could write a poem only you would read,

and that John Q. Public would catch wind of this intimacy

somehow, and somehow they would reward it

handsomely enough that I could go on doing nothing but writing poems

addressed to and seen only by you but

sung of by others with such veneration that successive classes of

undergraduates would write embarrassingly earnest research papers

numerating their hopes for what said poems contain

without their ever actually wanting to see the poems themselves.

Even TMZ would get in on the act,

shooing its cameras elsewhere. Oh! That is what I want,

to make you what the world adores through its unknowing.

Constants are rare enough to cherish.

Here, like the bread I burn each morning, I lay

an offering out for you by hand. That my blood

revels in this recurrence. That my blood

lingers in its tunnels

in the full belief that this is how blood stops time.

Even my blood has theories!

Constants are rare enough to cherish.

Like constellations, they are mostly what you make of them.

All the words in a love poem mean the same thing:
Reverence stopped here; here at the river of my blood.
Kneeling, it drank and became the river.

NOTES

"Pseudo-Martyr": The poem takes its title from John Donne's prose work of the same name.

"Mr. Dreamy": The quoted text comes from Charles M. Oliver's *Critical Companion to Walt Whitman: A Literary Reference to His Life and Work.* New York: Facts on File, 2006.

"My last conversation with Mary Jane Bailey": The poem references quotations included in Robert Archambeau's "Hating the Other Kind of Poetry." *Copper Nickel* 21, Fall 2015.

"The Loves in a Word Poem All Mean the Same Thing": The italicized line comes from John Donne's "The Broken Heart."

"After Catullus": The first line is adapted from Charles Martin's translation of Catullus's poem "#8."

ACKNOWLEDGMENTS

Generous thanks to the publications where these poems first appeared.

The Adroit Journal; Bellingham Review; The Bennington Review; Blackbird; Cherry Tree; The Collagist; Crab Orchard Review; Forklift, OH; Kenyon Review Online; Memorious; Nashville Review; New England Review; The Paris-American; Pleiades; Ploughshares; Southern Indiana Review; Sycamore Review; Threepenny Review; Thrush; Waccamaw; West Branch; and *Western Humanities Review.*

"Amateur Hour (What Do Sad Songs Remind You Of)" and "Elegy to a Black Bear Head Poorly Stuffed and Mounted" both also appeared on versedaily.org.

Thank you, everyone, for your guidance, support, friendship, and patience; especially: Sue Clark, John Clark, Peter Clark, Rachel Farley, Lucy Clark, Oliver Clark, Andrew Clark, Mary Buitrago, Paul Buitrago, Isabel Buitrago, Dylan Buitrago, Sasha West, Zadie West-Clark, Taffy Kim, Martin Kim, Doug West; Elizabeth Arnold, Michael Collier, Blas Falconer, Jennifer Grotz, Matt Hart, Joan Houlihan, Phillis Levin, Carl Phillips, Stanley Plumly, Joshua Weiner; Aaron Balkan, Clare Banks, Paul Bolstad, Katy Didden, Emari DiGiorgio, Robin Ekiss, Tarfia Faizullah, Mary Alice Fallon Yeskey, Christian Anton Gerard, James Allen Hall, Leslie Harrison, Shara Lessley, Joshua Mensch, Jill Meyers, Ian Miller, Sean Miller, Brian Nicolet, Damien Ober, Joanna Osborne, Paul Otremba, Duncan Primeaux, Michele Reese,

Stephen Reichert, Jason Schneiderman, Kate Singer, Tyler Stoddard Smith, Mary Helen Specht, Avery Slater, Alison Stine, Ian Varley, Tiphanie Yanique, Shannon Zangs; Martha Rhodes, Ryan Murphy, Four Way Books; The English Department and Creative Writing Program at the University of Maryland, College Park; The Bread Loaf Writers' Conference; The Colrain Conference.

This project is supported in part by an award from the National Endowment for the Arts.

Charlie Clark studied poetry at the University of Maryland. His poems have appeared in *New England Review, Ploughshares, Threepenny Review, West Branch,* and elsewhere. He lives in Austin, Texas.

Publication of this book was made possible by grants and donations. We are also grateful to those individuals who participated in our 2019 Build a Book Program. They are:

Anonymous (14), Sally Ball, Vincent Bell, Jan Bender-Zanoni, Laurel Blossom, Adam Bohannon, Lee Briccetti, Jane Martha Brox, Anthony Cappo, Carla & Steven Carlson, Andrea Cohen, Janet S. Crossen, Marjorie Deninger, Patrick Donnelly, Charles Douthat, Morgan Driscoll, Lynn Emanuel, Blas Falconer, Monica Ferrell, Joan Fishbein, Jennifer Franklin, Sarah Freligh, Helen Fremont & Donna Thagard, Ryan George, Panio Gianopoulos, Lauri Grossman, Julia Guez, Naomi Guttman & Jonathan Mead, Steven Haas, Bill & Cam Hardy, Lori Hauser, Bill Holgate, Deming Holleran, Piotr Holysz, Nathaniel Hutner, Elizabeth Jackson, Rebecca Kaiser Gibson, Dorothy Tapper Goldman, Voki Kalfayan, David Lee, Howard Levy, Owen Lewis, Jennifer Litt, Sara London & Dean Albarelli, David Long, Ralph & Mary Ann Lowen, Jacquelyn Malone, Fred Marchant, Donna Masini, Louise Mathias, Catherine McArthur, Nathan McClain, Richard McCormick, Kamilah Aisha Moon, James Moore, Beth Morris, John Murillo & Nicole Sealey, Kimberly Nunes, Rebecca Okrent, Jill Pearlman, Marcia & Chris Pelletiere, Maya Pindyck, Megan Pinto, Barbara Preminger, Kevin Prufer, Martha Rhodes, Paula Rhodes, Silvia Rosales, Linda Safyan, Peter & Jill Schireson, Jason Schneiderman, Roni & Richard Schotter, Jane Scovell, Andrew Seligsohn & Martina Anderson, Soraya Shalforoosh, Julie A. Sheehan, James Snyder & Krista Fragos, Alice St. Claire-Long, Megan Staffel, Marjorie & Lew Tesser, Boris Thomas, Pauline Uchmanowicz, Connie Voisine, Martha Webster & Robert Fuentes, Calvin Wei, Bill Wenthe, Allison Benis White, Michelle Whittaker, Rachel Wolff, and Anton Yakovlev.